For
Lucien, Basile
Malo, Pablo
& Valentina

CITIES

Manon Bucciarelli

Translated by
JOSEPHINE MURRAY

HC
CB
HARPERCOLLINS
CHILDREN'S BOOKS

DID YOU KNOW THAT...

cities haven't always existed? For a long time, humans lived nomadically, travelling with their herds of animals according to the seasons. Then they settled in farms. The first cities were built along rivers, and their founders were often merchants, who were soon joined by craftspeople – blacksmiths, bakers, and artisans – offering their services to whoever needed them. Cities and towns, known as urban areas, developed because people with similar needs came together to share resources and agreed to follow rules that helped everyone live together successfully.

From Paris to Miami and Bamako to Tokyo, whether standing by the sea or nestled in the mountains, every city has its own history, architecture, transport, food, culture and festivals that give it its individual character, depending on the climate, environment and resources surrounding it.

By discovering all these cities, we are celebrating the people of the world, the ingenuity and creativity of their construction, their organisation and, above all, the wonderful ways in which they live together!

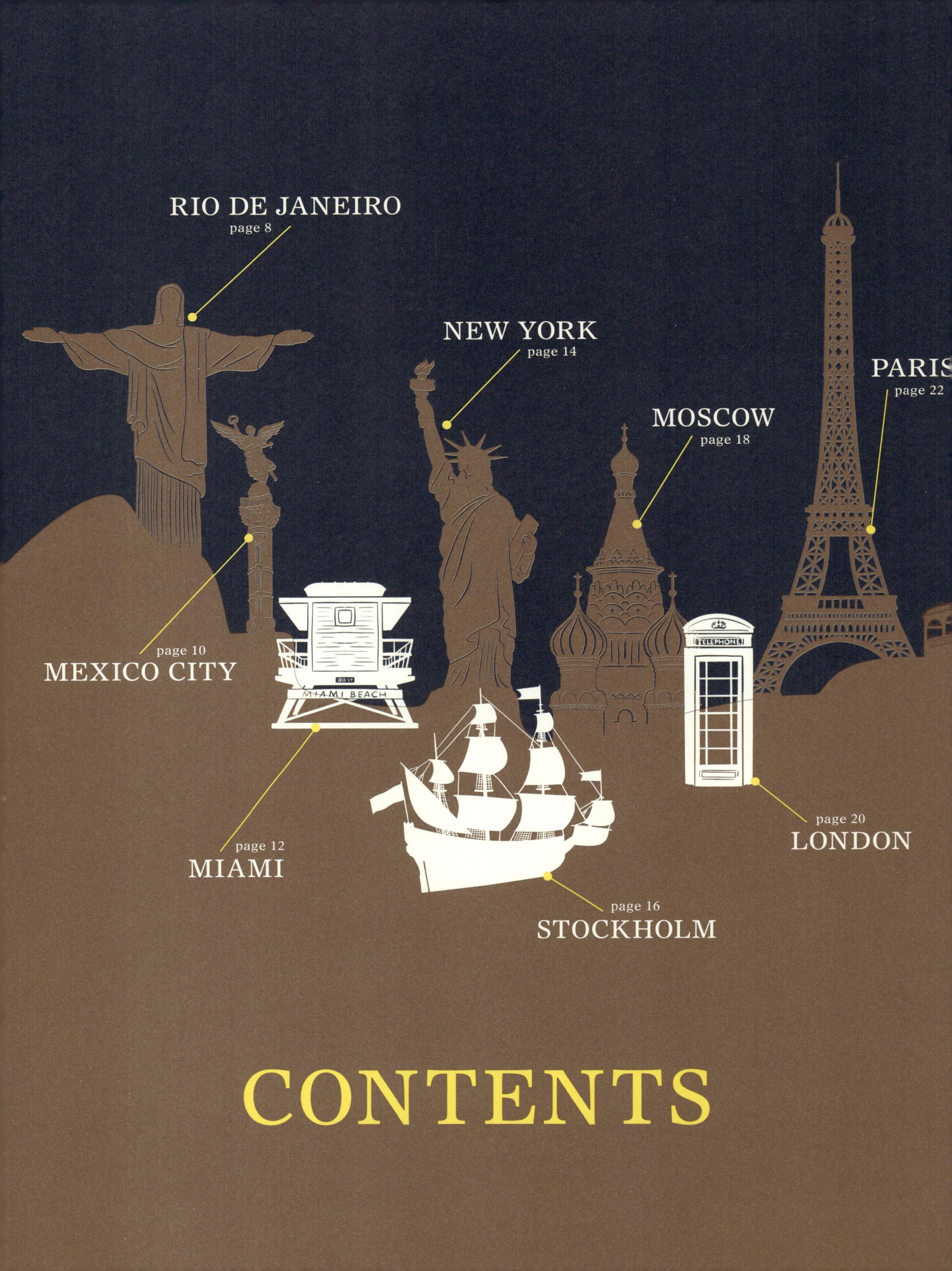

CONTENTS

In this book, you'll discover 16 cities of the world.
Each one has its own famous streets, museums, monuments,
districts, styles, ways of life and distinctive sounds.

Through these pages, you'll be able to find out about the
history of these cities and feel like you are really there!

Towering above the entrance to Guanabara Bay, this huge granite rock is almost 400 metres above sea level. Visitors reach its summit on a cable car that was installed over a century ago. Its rounded shape, typical of sugar blocks, inspired its name . . .

SUGAR LOAF MOUNTAIN

•

He stands at the summit of Mount Corcovado, his outstretched arms forming a cross. Completed in 1931, this Art Deco-style monument is 30 metres tall. Demonstrating the importance of the Catholic religion in the lives of Brazilians, he is known as . . .

CHRIST THE REDEEMER

•

Famous all over the world, it's the most eagerly anticipated event of the year. The first one took place in 1723. The star attraction is the parade, with everyone playing their part: musicians, flag-bearers, masters of ceremony and dancers. It's the . . .

RIO CARNIVAL

RIO DE JANEIRO

This yellow-coloured object symbolises a region in the hills of Rio de Janeiro. It first opened in 1877 and was originally pulled by horses before the arrival of electricity. Linking the city centre to the Santa Teresa district, it's the . . .

SANTA TERESA TRAM

•

Whether salty or sweet, it's surprisingly light! Sold by street vendors on the beach or in traffic jams, this crunchy, ring-shaped biscuit is beloved by the city's residents. Its paper packaging features a funny character with a globe-shaped head. It's the . . .

BISCOITO GLOBO

•

Linking the Lapa and Santa Teresa districts, it has over 200 steps decorated with tiles in the colours of the Brazilian flag – yellow, green and blue. Named after the artist who created it, it's the . . .

SELARÓN STAIRCASE

Its leaves unfurl in plumes along its twisting branches, and its large flowers bloom in spring, like a spectacular firework display! As the petals fall, they cover the streets of Mexico City with a purple carpet. This tree is known as the 'blue flamboyant' or . . .

JACARANDA

Once used for transporting goods, today these colourful vessels carry tourists along the canals of the Xochimilco district, accompanied by the music of the mariachis who play on board. This large, flat-bottomed boat is called a . . .

TRAJINERA

MEXICO CITY

TROPICAL
Fruteria

This column was put up to celebrate Mexico's independence after three centuries of Spanish rule. The goddess Nike at its summit spreads her wings above one of Mexico City's longest avenues. Cast from bronze, she's completely covered in 24-carat gold and holds a laurel wreath, a symbol of victory. It's the . . .

ANGEL OF INDEPENDENCE

AV
5 D

People come here to buy fruit served in small jars, along with pineapple, mango or guava juice, all for just a few pesos. In Spanish it's often called the 'carrito de frutas'. It's a . . .

FRUIT CART

BIENVENIDO

MEXICO ★ DESCONOCIDO

A gigantic building with a curved shape, it's entirely covered in small metal hexagons. Inside is the incredible collection of paintings and sculptures of a wealthy Mexican businessman who named it after his wife. It's the . . .

SOUMAYA MUSEUM

Mainly built of marble, it's so heavy that its foundations are gradually sinking into the ground. It has a spectacular golden dome and contains huge murals by artists including Diego Rivera. Used as a theatre, opera house and museum, it's the . . .

PALACIO DE BELLAS ARTES

Located at the heart of the Latin Quarter, Little Havana, this place is a must-see at any time of day. Here, people play lively games of dominoes to the sound of salsa music. Created to commemorate a Cuban revolutionary, it's known as Máximo Gómez Park, or simply . . .

DOMINO PARK

Created in 1965 as the home of the future by designer Richard Buckminster Fuller, its spherical shape is inspired by a fly's eye. Located in Miami's Design District, it's the . . .

FLY'S EYE DOME

PARK

NT

This art installation fits in with the rest of the fantastic museums, sublime murals and spectacular sculptures of Miami! Acquired by The Bass Museum of Art, this stack of colourful rocks by artist Ugo Rondinone is called . . .

MIAMI MOUNTAIN

Sitting on top of stilts, it looks down onto the beach so the lifeguards can keep an eye on the swimmers and surfers who go into the waves. Built in typical Miami Art Deco style with vibrant colours and geometric shapes, this little tower is called a . . .

LIFEGUARD TOWER

80st

MIAMI BEACH

MIAMI

All along Miami Beach, facing the Atlantic, it's made up of more than 800 Art Deco-style buildings constructed between 1920 and 1943. They're all painted in pastel shades that emphasise their geometric shapes, giving a stylish appearance to the district known as . . .

ART DECO DISTRICT

Before this structure was built, it was impossible to cross the East River without a boat. At just over a mile long, it's one of the first suspension bridges in the United States. It links Manhattan to Brooklyn. It's the . . .

BROOKLYN BRIDGE

•

A New York avenue famous for being the heart of American theatre, it attracts millions of theatregoers each year. Lit up by sparkling signs and illuminated show posters, it's known for hosting the best musicals and theatre performances. It's . . .

BROADWAY

•

Standing at 319 metres, this building, with its iconic pointed spire, may not reach the heights of the nearby Empire State Building, but it captivates with its Art Deco design. This architectural masterpiece combines angular shapes and curved lines. It's the . . .

CHRYSLER BUILDING

NEW YORK

In the past, this statue was like a beacon, welcoming travellers who crossed the Atlantic. This figure, with her raised arm, crown and draped toga, was designed by French sculptor Frédéric-Auguste Bartholdi. It's the. . .

STATUE OF LIBERTY

•

Planted on the moon in 1969, this is one of the world's most famous flags. Its red and white stripes symbolise the first 13 states that founded the American Union. Its blue rectangle then received a new star each time a new state joined the Union, and they now number 50. It's known as Old Glory or . . .

THE STARS AND STRIPES

•

Used by hundreds of thousands of passengers every day, it has a huge vaulted concourse with a clock. With four white glass faces, its time is set forward by one minute, giving passengers an extra 60 seconds to say goodbye. It's the biggest train station in the world, it's . . .

GRAND CENTRAL TERMINAL

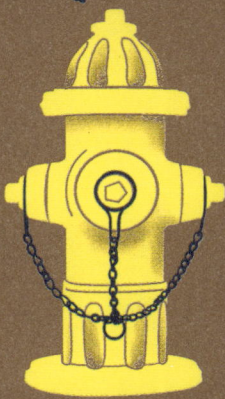

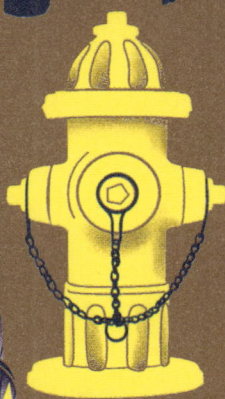

NYSTEKT STRÖMMING

Almost 400 years ago, it capsized and sank on its maiden voyage. After 333 years underwater, it was finally discovered by a researcher who specialised in shipwrecks. It is the best-preserved 17th-century ship in the world. Its name is . . .

VASA

STOC KHOL M

Herring, salmon, venison and elk sausage – you'll find the best Swedish food here! Built in the 19th century, this food market is full of pretty carved wooden stalls bursting with fresh produce. Even the king's cooks shop here! It's . . .

ÖSTERMALMS SALUHALL

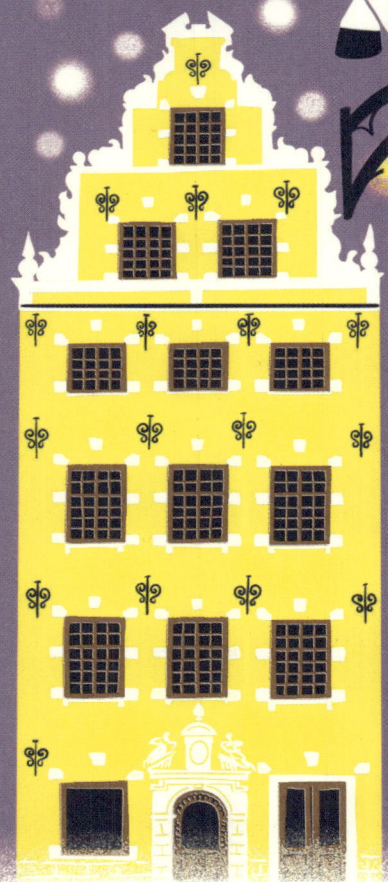

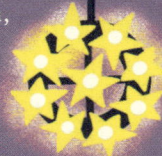

SKA

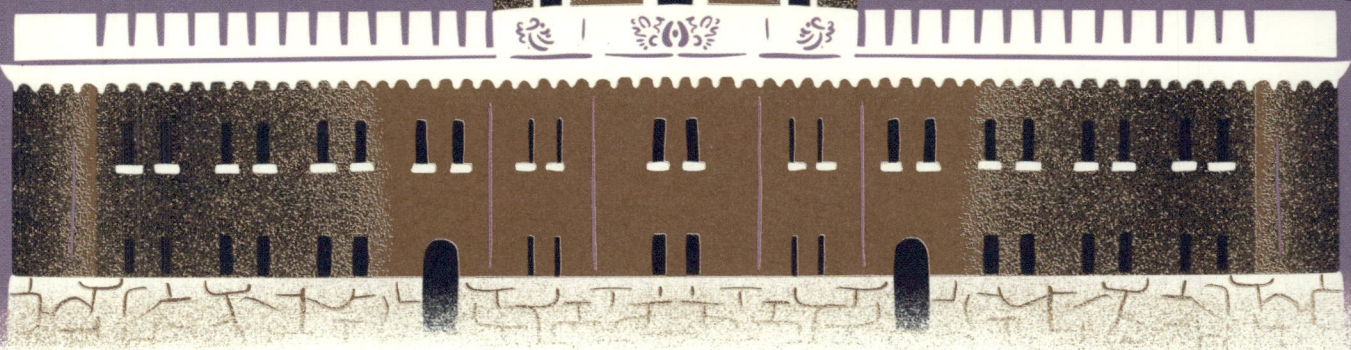

NYSTEKT STRÖMMING

Located by the waterside at Royal Djurgården, in the very heart of the capital, this is part of Princess Estelle's sculpture collection. Made up of rings tied together, it's called . . .

LIFE RINGS

Standing on the islet of Kastellholmen, it looks like a small castle. Guarding the entrance of the harbour, it has long been a military building, from which passing ships were saluted with cannon blasts. It's . . .

KASTELLET

SEN

84

M SEGER
EFTR.

coinciding with the summer solstice, his is a celebration of life and love. wedish people wear flower crowns d dance around maypoles. It's the ngest day of the year and the sun only oes down for a short time. It's . . .

MIDSUMMER

Rolled or plaited and baked golden brown, it is sprinkled with sugar and flavoured with cinnamon. It can be enjoyed at any time of day with a coffee, for a comforting break called Fika. Known worldwide as a cinnamon roll, in Swedish it's called a . . .

KANELBULLE

КРАСНАЯ ПЛОЩАДЬ

ЛАВРУ...
ПЕ...

He visits at Orthodox Christmas, which takes place on 7 January. It's the biggest festival of the year, and the whole country is decorated with fairy lights to prepare for his arrival and celebrate the New Year. He gives presents to Russian children, who call him Grandfather Frost or . . .

DED MOROZ

Made in the 18th century from 200 tons of bronze, it was partially broken during a fire. Today it sits at the foot of Ivan the Great Bell Tower in the Kremlin's Cathedral Square. It's known as the . . .

TSAR BELL

First introduced in Prague and then brought to Moscow in the 1960s, this was a popular way to get around the city. It's the tramway . . .

TATRA T3

НСКИЙ

MOSCOW

It was built in Red Square from
1555 to 1561 on the orders of
Ivan the Terrible, the first tsar
of Russia. Its nine multicoloured
bulb-shaped domes are typical of
Orthodox architecture. It houses
the tomb of St Basil the Blessed,
from whom it gets its name . . .

ST BASIL'S
CATHEDRAL

Built for the Russian pavilion at the 1937 Paris World Fair, it stands
24 metres tall! Made of steel, this huge sculpture of a man and a
woman – a worker and a farmer holding a sickle and hammer – is called . . .

WORKER AND KOLKHOZ WOMAN

A regular sight on the streets of London. You can climb the stairs to its top deck in front of St Paul's Cathedral, then jump off its rear platform in Trafalgar Square! It's the famous red double-decker . . .

LONDON BUS

Discovered stranded on a beach in Ireland in 1891, it hangs in the great hall of London's Natural History Museum. At 25.2 metres long, it's as big as the diplodocus skeleton it replaced. It's a blue whale skeleton called . . .

HOPE

TELEPHONE

It spans the River Thames with its two square towers. Thanks to its bascule system that operates like a drawbridge, it opens in two halves to allow even the largest boats to pass through. Pedestrians can go up to the upper galleries to admire the view! It's . . .

TOWER BRIDGE

LON DON

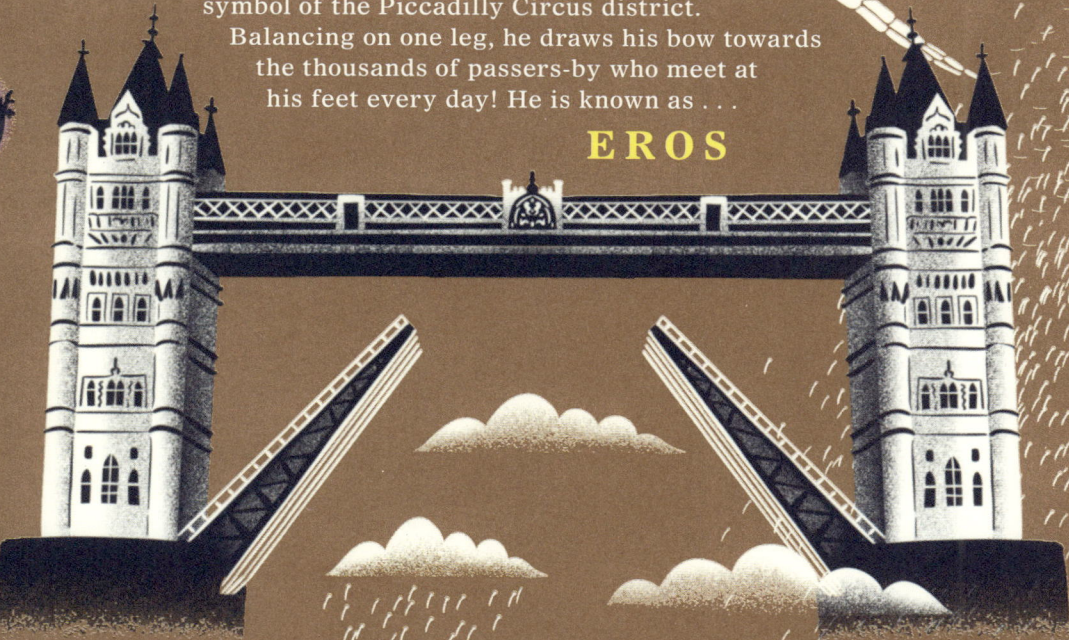

In pride of place atop a fountain, he's the symbol of the Piccadilly Circus district. Balancing on one leg, he draws his bow towards the thousands of passers-by who meet at his feet every day! He is known as . . .

EROS

Its gothic style gives it a sense of majesty, just like the rest of the Palace of Westminster of which it forms a part. All four of its sides are dominated by the faces of a huge clock and its official name is the Elizabeth Tower. But it's most famous for housing an enormous bell, which weighs almost 14 tons and is nicknamed . . .

BIG BEN

Opened in 2000, it's the largest cantilevered observation wheel in the world. Once inside one of its capsules, passengers soar 135 metres into the air, which gives them a view over the city, from the Palace of Westminster to Waterloo Station! It's the . . .

LONDON EYE

Built of cast iron and glass in the early 20th century, these Art Nouveau-style structures show travellers the way into the metro/underground railway. You'll find the best examples at the stations of Porte Dauphine and Abbesses. Sharing their name with their creator, they are . . .

GUIMARD MÉTRO ENTRANCES

8me ARR^t

AVENUE DES CHAMPS-ÉLYSÉES

Built for the World Exhibition in 1889, it was the tallest tower in the world for over 40 years! Its four 'feet' are firmly fixed more than 7 metres into the ground to support the 10,000-ton weight of its metal structure. Symbol of the capital and nicknamed the 'Iron Lady', it's the . . .

EIFFEL TOWER

METROPOLITAIN

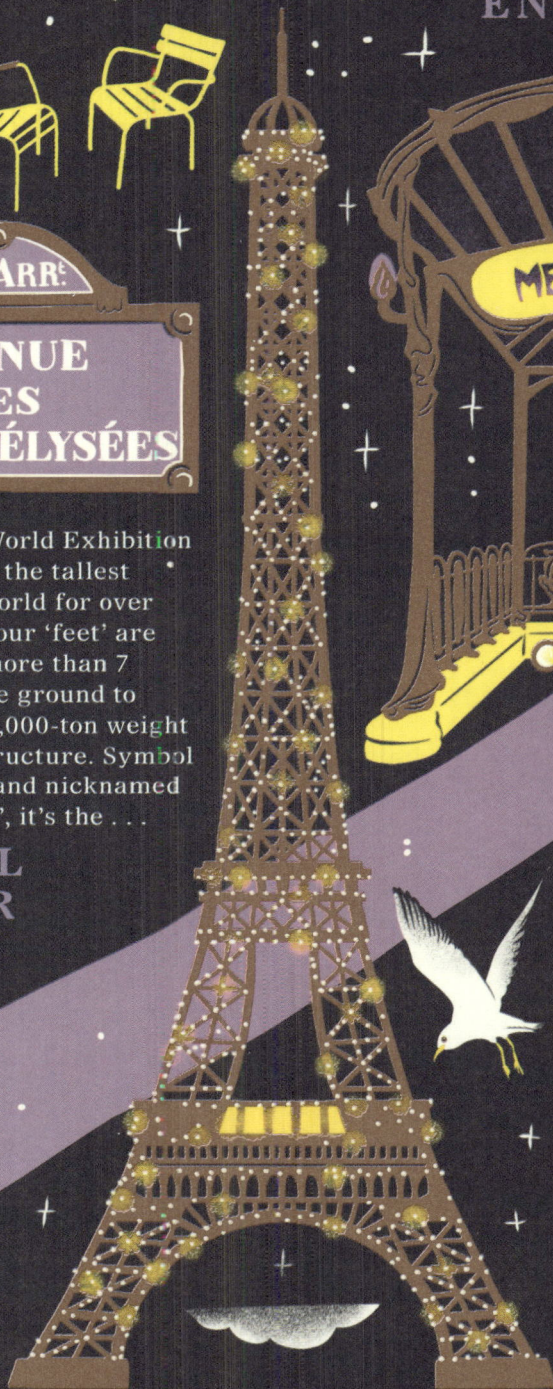

PARIS

Shows at the Moulin-Rouge, Théâtre du Châtelet, Cirque d'Hiver, Trianon, Olympia and the Folies Bergère, have livened up Parisian nightlife for a long time. These structures were created 150 years ago to display posters, so that no one would miss seeing these wonderful spectacles. Still in use today, they are . . .

MORRIS COLUMNS

GERIE

DULUC
DÉTECTIVE

Created in 1872, these
provided people with
free access to drinking
water. Embellished with
four sculptures symbolising
Charity, Kindness,
Simplicity and Sobriety,
their name comes from
their inventor, Sir Richard
Wallace. They are . . .

WALLACE FOUNTAINS

patisserie
confiseries

PH

Napoleon I was crowned emperor in the choir of
this building. Framed by two tall square towers,
its Gothic facade is decorated with an enormous
rose window above the main entrance. Its many
gargoyles were added in the Middle Ages and
made famous by author Victor Hugo. It is . . .

NOTRE-DAME CATHEDRAL

4me ARR.

PLACE DES VOSGES

AL VAPORETTO

OSTERIA DEL GASON

HOTEL IRIS

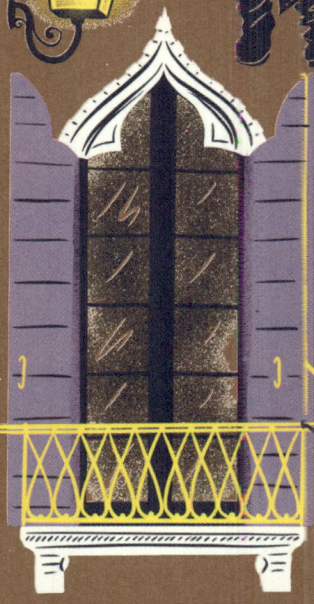

This structure spans the Grand Canal, linking two of the city's districts, which were separated from each other before it was built at the end of the 16th century. More than just a place for people to cross the canal, it has shops along both sides of its arches. Built in the style of the Ponte Vecchio in Florence, it's the . . .

RIALTO BRIDGE

•

Soft and fleshy, it's smaller and has fewer prickly leaves than the common green artichoke. Its unique flavour and beautiful violet colour come from the fertile clay and salt soil of the island of Sant'Erasmo, where it's grown. The Venetians love to eat it raw with a little garlic. It is a . . .

PURPLE ARTICHOKE

•

This world-famous event, known for the magnificent masks and costumes worn by people taking part, has been running for almost a thousand years! It takes place in winter for about ten days during which the city transforms into a gigantic parade of elegant characters and popular figures such as Colombina, Pulcinella and Harlequin. It's the . . .

VENICE CARNIVAL

VEN ICE

Facing the Doge's Palace, it rises above the rooftops to a height of almost 100 metres. Built where it's thought there was once a watchtower, in the past this building was a lighthouse. Later, Galileo used it as an observatory, but its main purpose is to be the bell tower of St Mark's Basilica. It's the . . .

ST MARK'S CAMPANILE

•

These are the visible parts of an ingenious system of rainwater collection wells, set up by the Republic of Venice to ensure the city had its own supply of drinking water. Beautifully sculpted and placed in the centre of a square, they are raised up on a few steps to avoid being submerged during high tides (acqua alta). They are known as the . . .

VERE DA POZZO

•

This animal can be seen everywhere – on coats of arms, coins, seals, bas-relief sculptures, the facades of churches and on monuments. It represents St Mark, patron saint of Venice since the 9th century. It has wings and holds an open book, a symbol of peace, between its paws. It's . . .

ST MARK'S LION

Each souk, a vast labyrinth of market stalls, has its own speciality: jewellery, spices, lanterns, baskets, slippers or fabrics. One souk is overflowing with carpets from various regions of the country and in a wide range of colours, patterns and textures, it's the famous . . .

JOUTIA ZRABI

Built in 1929, it mixes traditional Moroccan architecture with Art Deco style. Both a home and artist's studio, it has distinctive ultramarine-blue walls highlighted with yellow. It's surrounded by a large garden teeming with cacti, bamboo and jasmine. It is decorated with ponds and fountains. It was created by the French painter Jacques Majorelle. It's the . . .

VILLA MAJORELLE

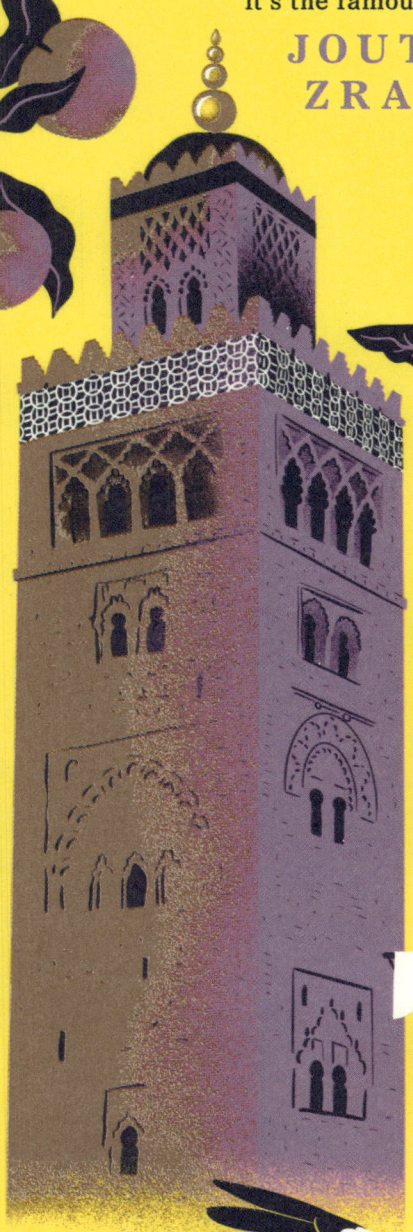

قف

Passed down through families and set up in the heart of the famous Jemaa el-Fna Square, these provide a meeting place for local people from early morning until late into the night. Loaded with clementines, grapefruits, oranges or lemons, depending on the season, they are . . .

ORANGE JUICE CARTS

First used in Morocco a thousand years ago, these small glazed ceramic pieces are traditionally coloured green, blue, brown, yellow or white. Made in a variety of shapes, they are put together to form geometric patterns. They decorate the floors and walls of riads, mosques, hammams and palaces. Depending on the region, they're called 'zliz', 'jelliz' or . . .

ZELLIGE

MAR RAKE CH

Measuring 77 metres high, its minaret is decorated in typical Arab-Andalusian style. Five times a day, the voice of the muezzin rises from its summit to call Muslim people to prayer. Built in the former booksellers' quarter, it's the city's largest mosque, and its name means 'bookseller'. It's the . . .

KUTUBIYYA

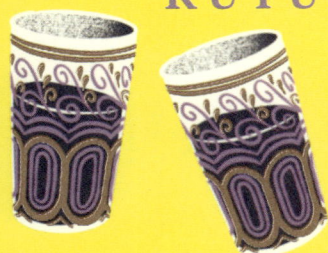

You can see his red suit and flamboyant hat and hear his bell ringing as he walks towards the souks or round the squares of the medina. He carries large goatskin pouches filled with fresh water, which in the past he delivered to shopkeepers and passers-by in exchange for money. Relic of a bygone era when running water didn't yet exist, he's a water seller, known in Marrakech as a . . .

GUERRAB

At the heart of the city, this is a souk where you can find mangoes, fish, djembes (traditional drums), jewellery and fabrics. Standing in the centre of Bamako's big market, its pink geometric shapes are typical of Malinese mud-brick architecture. It's known as the . . .

PINK MARKET

•

They are all green, but their owners decorate them in unique ways so each has its own personality. Whether they're carrying two or twenty Bamako residents, they drive at a steady pace to keep the roads safe! They're the minibus taxis known as . . .

SOTRAMAS

•

With its gigantic arms reaching towards the sky, holding up a globe with a white dove perched on top, it symbolises national unity and the return of peace to Mali. It's the . . .

PEACE MONUMENT

BAMAKO

You'll find one in every home in Bamako! This kettle-shaped object is used in the bathroom, not the kitchen. Made of coloured plastic, it can hold around three litres of water and is used for washing. It's a . . .

TASSALÉ

•

This concrete structure is covered in marble, and has four large arches sheltering a torch, a symbol of freedom. On its pillars you can read the names of the heroes who made Mali's independence possible after a century of colonisation. It's the . . .

MONUMENT OF INDEPENDENCE

•

An iconic national drink, this is sold everywhere on the streets of Bamako, and it is much loved by Malians. It's usually made at home from the fruit of the baobab tree, it is . . .

BOUYE JUICE

This district in the European part of the city is unique because of the architecture of its Ottoman houses and its steep, cobbled alleyways. Some of the multicoloured fronts of its buildings are 200 years old, which has earned it UNESCO World Heritage status. It's the district called . . .

BALAT

Built in the 6th century to store rainwater, this underground chamber is larger than a football pitch. Its vaulted ceiling is supported by 336 marble columns, two of which are decorated with a mysterious head of Medusa. It's the . . .

BASILICA CISTERN

Protected by high ramparts, this enormous palace was home to the sultan and his court for several centuries. It was built after the fall of Constantinople in 1459. Made up of many buildings, patios and gardens, it is now a museum. It houses the remains of the acropolis (fortress) of Byzantium, many treasures of the Ottoman Empire, and a number of strange, centuries-old trees with hollow trunks. It's the imperial palace of . . .

TOPKAPI

This delicious bread roll, both soft like a brioche and crusty, is shaped like a ring and covered with sesame seeds. It's sold in streets all over the city by salespeople carrying large trays on their heads, who shout 'Taze simit!' which means 'fresh bread'. Others use pretty red and white carts. It's a . . .

SIMIT

Hanging from rearview mirrors of taxi cabs, on doorhandles, necklaces and keyrings, it's everywhere! This eye-shaped talisman is designed to protect from evil and is usually made of deep blue and white glass. It's the . . .

EVIL EYE

TAKSİM

İETT DURAĞI

TRT İSTANBUL RADYOSU

ISTANBUL

SİMİTÇİ 18

BEYOĞLU

You can see its silhouette through the morning mist and hear the sound of its engine amid the cries of seagulls. It sails on the Bosphorus, from Asia to Europe, linking the two shores of the city. People prefer it to the traffic jams on the bridges and enjoy the journey with a Turkish coffee or hot milk. It's a ferry, or a . . .

VAPUR

223

ASILMAK YAGAK YE TEHLİKELİDİR

Related to the Indian carnation, its many petals are shaped like yellow, orange or white pompoms. Grown all over the country, these flowers are often made into garlands or necklaces called 'mala' and hung up in temples and homes. It's the . . .

MARIGOLD

This astronomical observatory was built in the 18th century. It includes the world's largest stone sundial, designed to measure time, predict eclipses and track planets. It's called . . .

JANTAR MANTAR

You'll easily spot its three wheels and yellow hood among the scooters! Traditionally, it was pulled by bicycle, but now it has a small engine and can carry two to four passengers. It's often called a 'tuk-tuk' or an . . .

AUTO RICKSHAW

This is one of the four gates that open onto the Garden of Lovers in Jaipur's City Palace. The Rose Gate represents winter, the Peacock Gate autumn and the Green Gate spring. This one represents summer. With its lintel lavishly decorated with lotus petals, it's the . . .

LOTUS GATE

JAIPUR

It stands at the entrance to a garden created on the country's largest roundabout. Its arches and walls are covered with hand-painted scenes illustrating Rajasthan's heritage. Decorated with colourful and gilded patterns, it is typical of the region's traditional architecture, it's the . . .

PATRIKA GATE

Made of bronze and weighing 250 tons, you can see this impressive statue from the bottom of the 268 steps leading up to it. Pilgrims are welcomed by its serene face and spiritual hand gestures – the hand on its knee is palm upwards to symbolise generosity. It's the . . .

TIAN TAN BUDDHA

•

Created in the style of the Tang dynasty, this garden contains many species of trees and bonsai. People walk along the paths to admire the fish swimming in its ponds and see the famous 'Pavilion of Absolute Perfection', which is made of wood, painted yellow and green. It's the . . .

NAN LIAN GARDEN

•

This large golden sculpture was put up in the middle of a square to commemorate the end of British rule in Hong Kong in 1997. A ceremony is held in front of it every morning to raise the flag of Hong Kong alongside the flag of China. It represents a Bauhinia blakeana, or the Hong Kong orchid tree, but because it looks a bit like a cabbage, people call it the . . .

GOLDEN BAUHINIA

HONG KONG

This dance is traditionally performed to celebrate Lunar New Year. Two dancers hidden under a large costume move together to give the illusion of being a four-legged animal. The dancer at the back can't see anything, so they are guided by the dancer in front, who wears a huge mask. It's the . . .

LION DANCE

•

These make it possible for people to walk safely above the streets, so they don't have to wait when they want to cross a road. They connect several buildings and tram stations. A vast above-ground pedestrian network, they are the . . .

CENTRAL ELEVATED WALKWAYS

•

It looks tiny and very old among the modern skyscrapers nearby! But it has stood here proudly for over a century, even though the station it used to overlook has been moved. Made of red brick and granite, it survived the Battle of Hong Kong during World War II and still tells the time today. It's the . . .

FORMER KOWLOON-CANTON RAILWAY CLOCK TOWER

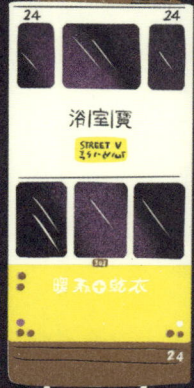

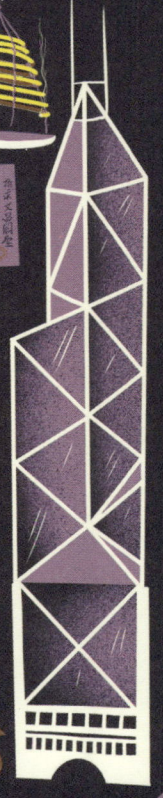

カラオケ

歌広場

Hung up every year to
celebrate Children's Day in
Japan, these long streamers
are made of paper or fabric
in the shape of koi carp.
Displayed in groups of
three or more to represent
members of the same
family, they're called . . .

KOINOORI

郵便
POST

This tasty broth is
garnished with noodles,
dried seaweed, grilled
pork, chives, egg
and sometimes a
narutomaki fishcake.
You'll find it for sale
in small mobile food
stalls called 'yatai'.
It's the delicious . . .

RAMEN

TOKYO

From the observation deck on its second floor, you can see Mount Fuji to the southwest of the city. Three metres taller than the Eiffel Tower, it's a symbol of Japan's reconstruction after World War II. It's the . . .

TOKYO TOWER

カラオケ 歌広場

This statue is not far from Shibuya's bustling famous pedestrian crossroads. Facing the nearby underground railway exit that shares its name, it honours a faithful dog, who waited for his master there every day for ten years. It's . . .

HACHIKŌ

In Tokyo, you'll find one on every street corner or next to other vending machines. It works around the clock, selling a wide range of refreshing drinks and instant meals. Its name means 'vending machine'. It's a 'jidohanbaiki' or simply . . .

JIHANKI

This gate is used to reach the oldest Buddhist temple in Tokyo, the Sensōji. Measuring more than 11 metres high, it contains statues of the Shinto gods Fūjin and Raijin, as well as a traditional red lantern on which its name is inscribed. It's the Thunder Gate, or . . .

KAMINARIMON

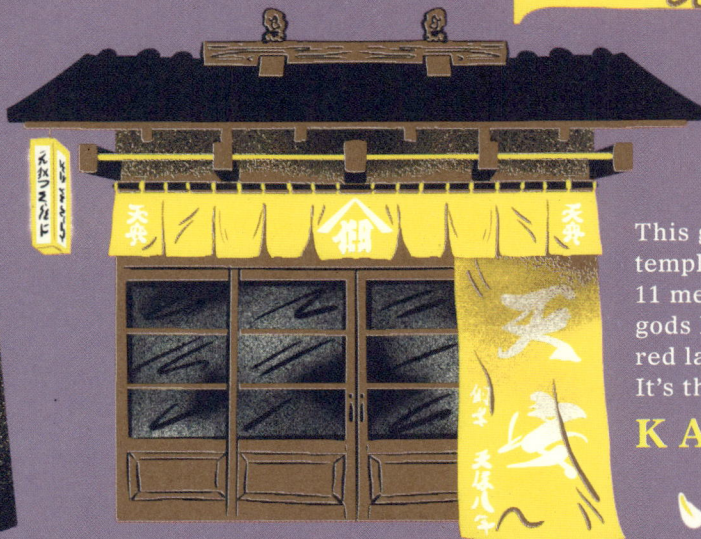

Sydney's residents come here for fairground rides, fun and candyfloss! It opened in 1935 and although it has been renovated many times, it still has its original entrance of a head wearing a crown, inspired by the entrance to an older amusement park in Melbourne. It's . . .

LUNA PARK

SYDNEY

A golden cylinder on top of a very tall pillar, this structure is held in place by 56 cables securely attached to the ground. From its circular top floor, more than 250 metres above the ground, you get a panoramic view of the city. Also known as Centrepoint Tower, it's . . .

TOWER EYE

Built in 1858 following several fatal shipwrecks, this is one of the country's oldest lighthouses. Located at the tip of a rocky outcrop called South Head, its lantern warns sailors of the many reefs at the entrance to Sydney's huge harbour. This lighthouse with distinctive vertical red and white stripes is called . . .

HORNBY LIGHTHOUSE

Invented in 1922, this is made from brewer's yeast, has a very dark brown colour and a thick texture. Unlike chocolate spreads, this spread is salty! In Sydney, many people start their days full of vitamin B by eating a slice of buttered toast with . . .

VEGEMITE™

Famous all over the world for its unique shapes, this building was designed by a Danish architect and took 14 years to construct! Its large, pointed arches covered in cream and white tiles make it look like a boat in full sail. Its main concert hall houses the largest mechanical organ in the world, with over ten thousand pipes. It's the . . .

SYDNEY OPERA HOUSE

LUNA PARK

This is one of the widest bridges in the world. Connecting the districts of The Rocks and North Shore, it's one of the first steel-arch bridges ever built. It's the . . .

SYDNEY HARBOUR BRIDGE

FISHBURN

RIO DE JANEIRO (Brazil)

This metropolis of almost 7 million inhabitants is not the capital of Brazil, but its extraordinary carnival has made it the country's most famous city. Situated in the east of Brazil on the edge of the Atlantic Ocean, its indigenous peoples began trading with Europeans in the 16th century. Having colonised the areas around the famous beaches of Ipanema and Copacabana, the Portuguese founded the city in 1565 and named it 'January River'.

MEXICO CITY (Mexico)

The Aztecs founded Tenochtitlán, the capital of their empire, on one of the islands of Lake Texcoco in the heart of Mexico, on a high mountain plateau where several tectonic plates meet. Completely destroyed by the Spanish conquistadors in 1521, the city was rebuilt on the drained lake. Today this multicultural crossroads is home to over 22 million 'chilangos' (residents of Mexico City) who have revived its Aztec roots while combining them with Hispanic culture.

CHRIST THE REDEEMER
Created by Heitor da Silva Costa, Carlos Oswald, Paul Landowski and Gheorghe Leonida, finished in 1931.

SELARÓN STAIRCASE
A staircase with 215 steps, decorated with over 2,000 tiles and mirrors from 60 countries, created by Chilean artist, Jorge Selarón.

FLIP-FLOPS
Although strappy shoes were invented in Egypt, flip-flops as we know them today come from Brazil.

TRAJINERAS
Colourful boats which have been hand-made for centuries, often painted red and yellow.

BEETLE
This classic German Volkswagen model, designed by Ferdinand Porsche, has been popular in Mexico since the 1950s.

ANGEL OF INDEPENDENCE
A 45-metre-high column with a golden angel, put up in 1910 by Antonio Rivas Mercado to celebrate the centenary of Mexican independence.

BONDE ELÉTRICO
A type of public transport with iconic yellow tramcars, it was launched in the late 19th century but now has only two lines.

ORELHÕES
Egg-shaped telephone booths created in the early 1970s by Chinese-born designer, Chu Ming Silveira.

COPACABANA PAVEMENT
A pavement with a mosaic of black and white waves, created by landscape architect Roberto Burle Marx in the 1970s.

PALACIO DE BELLAS ARTES
The gilded dome of the Palace of Fine Arts, Mexico City's first opera house, was designed by Italian architect Adamo Boari and completed in 1934.

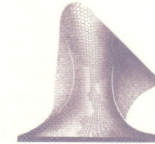

SOUMAYA MUSEUM
A museum founded by the businessman Carlos Slim and designed by architect Fernando Romero. Opened in 2011, it contains more than 65,000 works of art.

CALAVERAS
People create skulls painted with bright colours for the annual celebration of the Day of the Dead.

SUGAR LOAF MOUNTAIN
A 395-metre high granite monolith. It has been possible to reach its summit by cable car since 1912.

CAPOEIRA
A Brazilian dance-like martial art with 16th-century African roots, now a popular sport.

RIO CARNIVAL
A week-long, vibrant, festive and colourful parade with different schools of samba, started in 1723.

PRICKLY PEAR
A cactus native to Mexico, it appears on the Mexican flag. People eat its fruit and also its pads, 'nopalitos'.

LUCHA LIBRE
A kind of acrobatic Mexican wrestling style, practised since 1863 by luchadores (wrestlers) wearing masks.

JACARANDA
A tree native to South America which grows to around 15 metres tall, with fern-like leaves and purplish-blue flowers.

BISCOITO GLOBO
A ring-shaped biscuit invented by brothers Milton, Jaime and João Ponce in the 1950s.

BATUCADA
A percussive style of samba, usually played by a group on traditional instruments.

TOCO TOUCAN
This toucan lives in the Brazilian rainforest and savannah but can also be found at the tops of tall trees in the city of Rio de Janeiro.

FRUIT CART
A small, sometimes mobile fruit stand, typical of Mexico and Latin America.

FOOTBALL
The Brazilian national team has made football history by winning five World Cups with players such as Pelé, Ronaldo and Ronaldinho.

MIAMI (USA)

At the tip of Florida, in the southeast of the USA, Miami stretches along the Atlantic coast facing the Bahamas and Cuba. As a result, the city has a large Cuban community, which influences the city's culture, particularly its music and food. Miami is also famous for villas, turquoise swimming pools, white sandy beaches and palm trees, all bathed in sunshine and tropical warmth!

LIFEGUARD TOWERS
These 36 look-out towers in different shapes and colours, designed in an Art Deco-inspired style by William Lane, have been built since the 1990s.

ART DECO HISTORIC DISTRICT
There are 800 buildings in this famous South Beach district.

MIAMI MOUNTAIN
A 12.8-metre-high work of art by Swiss artist Ugo Rondinone, put up in Collins Park, South Beach in 2016.

FERRARI TESTAROSSA
Iconic vehicle from the Italian brand, manufactured from 1984 to 1996.

DOMINO PARK
Outdoor space which opened in 1976, where people play dominoes and chat with friends.

ROLLER SKATING
A fun and sporty activity. In Miami, people often skate to music on paths alongside the beaches.

GOLF
Known for its 14 golf courses, many people in Miami love to play golf in the sunshine.

FLY'S EYE DOME
Prototype of a futuristic spherical home dreamt up by inventor Richard Buckminster Fuller who wanted it to be eco-friendly and self-sufficient.

PINK FLAMINGO
This wading bird loves Florida and its marshes, as do herons, pelicans and egrets, which find plenty of food here.

NEW YORK (USA)

It has a population of 9 million and five famous boroughs (Manhattan, Brooklyn, Staten Island, the Bronx and Queens), but New York City is not the capital of the United States of America! Nicknamed the 'Big Apple', it's famous for its skyscrapers, built in the early 20th century on the Manhattan peninsula, which is surrounded by the Hudson and East Rivers. The symbolic Statue of Liberty has stood on a small island in the bay since 1886.

BROWNSTONES
Brick townhouses with distinctive metal fire escapes on their facades.

YELLOW TAXI CABS
The yellow colour of these vehicles became popular in New York City and the rest of the country.

FIRE HYDRANTS
Water supply points for fire engines, designed in 1863, probably by Frederick Graff.

TRAFFIC LIGHTS
The first traffic lights with three colours (previously traffic lights had only two colours) were invented in 1923 by self-taught engineer Garrett Augustus Morgan.

CHRYSLER BUILDING
A 77-storey skyscraper with a distinctive steel spire, built between 1928 and 1930, designed by architect William Van Alen.

STATUE OF LIBERTY
A 93-metre-high sculpture, designed and built between 1870 and 1884, which has watched over New York since 1886.

THE STARS AND STRIPES
Flag known for its 13 red and white stripes and 50 stars, thought to have been designed by politician Francis Hopkinson in 1776.

BROOKLYN BRIDGE
This bridge was built between 1869 and 1883, designed by engineer John Augustus Roebling, a master of suspension bridges.

HOT DOG
A Frankfurter sausage in a roll, often eaten with ketchup and mustard.

BROADWAY
Lined with over 40 theatres, Broadway runs for 21 km across Manhattan, which was originally a Native American trading place.

SQUIRRELS
There are 2,373 grey squirrels in Central Park, which is the most famous park in New York City.

GRAND CENTRAL STATION CLOCK
A clock designed by Henry Edward Bedford, famous for its four glass faces.

STOCKHOLM (Sweden)

Situated on the east coast of Sweden, Stockholm is on the Baltic Sea. Spread across 14 islands, it is an important port for Scandinavian maritime trade and became the country's capital in the 15th century. It is home to the royal palace where the monarch lives, as well as many museums, theatres, opera houses and universities, which all spread the cultural influence of this city throughout the world.

MOSCOW (Russia)

Located on the banks of the river from which it takes its name, Moscow is the capital of Russia. Its architecture demonstrates the enormous changes it has experienced during its history. With its fortified Kremlin, cathedrals from the time of the tsars, Soviet buildings, and commemorative statues glorifying the USSR (Union of Soviet Socialist Republics), this city has inspired many writers such as Jules Vernes and Leo Tolstoy.

TEKNISKA HÖGSKOLAN
Underground railway station of the Royal Institute of Technology, opened in 1973 to celebrate scientific and technological progress.

KANELBULLE
A traditional cinnamon-flavoured pastry, sold in every patisserie in Sweden and celebrated every year on 4 October.

VASA
Wreck of the warship, Vasa, which sank in 1628 on its maiden voyage; it is now on display in the museum named after it.

BOLSHOI THEATRE
Performance venue for ballet and operas, opened in 1825, and completely restored in 1856 after a fire.

TSAR BELL
Made of bronze, 6.60 metres in diameter and weighing 200 tons. It was damaged during a fire and has never been rung.

TRAMWAY
There has been a tramway in Moscow since 1899. Tatra T3 trams didn't arrive on the Moscow network until 1963.

KASTELLET
Fortress completed in 1848, built on the foundations of a military site dating from 1667. The Swedish flag is raised here every day.

GAMLA STAN
Historic centre of Stockholm, dating from the 13th century. A colourful district with cobbled streets, bustling with shops, cafés and museums.

ROYAL GUARD
Dressed in blue and white and often on horseback, the guards of Stockholm's royal palace parade every day.

MATRYOSHKA
Set of Russian dolls contained inside each other, created at the end of the 19th century.

MOSCOW KREMLIN
A group of cathedrals and palaces behind a fortified wall. It is the official seat of the Russian government.

DED MOROZ
The Russian equivalent of Father Christmas, often dressed in a blue coat, he brings gifts on the night of New Year's Eve, seven days before Orthodox Christmas.

SKANSEN
Open-air museum founded in 1891 by Arthur Hazelius, where farmhouses and houses show what daily life and traditions were like for Swedish people in the past.

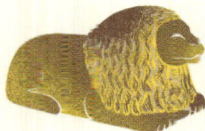

STONE LION
Protecting squares and pedestrian streets, these stone lions, symbols of the city, are also used as benches by Stockholm residents.

MIDSUMMER
Celebration of the summer solstice, when Swedish people get together to dance and share meals.

NOVOSLOBODSKAYA UNDERGROUND RAILWAY STATION
This station has 32 stained-glass windows designed by Pavel Korin, who was inspired by the patterns on traditional Russian clothing.

WORKER AND KOLKHOZ WOMAN
Commemorative sculpture created in 1937 by Russian artist Vera Mukhina.

ST BASIL'S CATHEDRAL
Built between 1555 and 1561, it overlooks Red Square; its multi-coloured 65-metre-high bulb-shaped domes were once golden.

RIDDARHOLMEN CHURCH
Stockholm's only medieval abbey, built in the early 14th century. It is where Swedish kings and queens are laid to rest.

LIFE RINGS
A 7.55-metre-high outdoor sculpture by Elmgreen & Dragset, consisting of lifebuoys attached together.

ÖSTERMALMS SALUHALL
Food market for local specialities built in 1888 by Isak Gustaf Clason and Kasper Salin.

BOLSHOI BALLET
Ballet company at the Bolshoi Theatre, where Tchaikovsky's *Swan Lake* was performed for the first time in 1877.

BEAR
The bear is the symbol of Russia, with around 300,000 of them in the country. There are three species: the brown bear, the polar bear and the Asiatic black bear.

LONDON (England)

The capital of England, London grew wealthy in the Middle Ages, thanks to its trade-friendly location on the River Thames. It has many famous sights including Buckingham Palace and the Tower of London. London is a lively and cosmopolitan city, where cultures from all over the world live alongside each other.

CHANGING THE GUARD

This parade of soldiers in red coats, with high bearskin helmets, takes place every morning outside Buckingham Palace.

TOWER BRIDGE

A bascule (lifting) bridge with two towers that is about 240 metres in length, designed by architects Sir Horace Jones and John Wolfe Barry and opened in 1894.

RED PHONE BOX

Phone booths designed by Sir Giles Gilbert Scott. They are an iconic symbol across the United Kingdom.

EROS

Bronze statue at Piccadilly Circus; erected in 1893 by Alfred Gilbert, in memory of politician and philanthropist Anthony Ashley Cooper, Earl of Shaftesbury.

LONDON BUS

Red double-decker bus used in London since the 1900s. The Routemaster, in use from 1956 to 2005, is the iconic version!

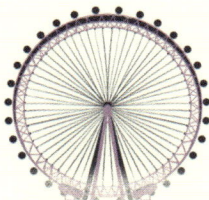

LONDON EYE

Observation wheel designed by Marks Barfield Architects built to celebrate the year 2000, hence its nickname: the Millennium Wheel.

RED FOX

A (not very) wild inhabitant of London, who finds food in rubbish bins and gardens. There are more than 10,000 in the city.

CAMDEN MARKET

Market in the Camden Town district which opened in 1974. Today it brings together a variety of independent shops.

HOPE

Blue whale skeleton on display in the Natural History Museum, made up of 221 bones and 25.2 metres long.

BIG BEN

The name of the bell that sits inside the Elizabeth Tower. The clock tower is about 97 metres tall.

THE SHARD

309-metre, 95-storey skyscraper, covered with 11,000 glass panels, designed by Renzo Piano and completed in 2012.

PARIS (France)

Built along the River Seine, it was called Lutetia during the time of the Roman Empire. It wasn't until the Middle Ages that it became the capital of France and took its present name. Its architecture was transformed by orders from Napoleon III and carried out by Baron Haussmann. The world-famous Eiffel Tower is its symbol.

GUIMARD MÉTRO ENTRANCES

Distinctive Art Nouveau-style entrances created around 1900 by Hector Guimard. There are only 88 out of 167 left standing.

HAUSSMAN BALCONIES

Balconies on the second and fifth floors of buildings, designed by urban planner Georges Eugène Haussmann for Napoleon III between 1852 and 1870.

MUSÉE D'ORSAY CLOCK

Gold clock created by Victor Laloux in 1900 and originally located in the hall of a railway station, which was converted into a museum in 1986.

STREET SIGNS

Originally made from enamelled lava stone for prefect Rambuteau in 1844, they are now made from metal with white letters on a background with green edging.

CROISSANTS

Laminated pastry inspired by an Austrian pastry called a 'kipferl'.

BUREN COLUMNS

Permanent display of 260 columns in the courtyard of the Palais-Royal, created by visual artist Daniel Buren in 1986.

LOUVRE PYRAMID

Glass and metal structure built between 1985 and 1989 by architect I.M.Pei, at the request of French president, François Mitterrand.

NOTRE-DAME

A cathedral on the Île de la Cité. Building began in 1163. It is a fine example of Gothic architecture. It was damaged by fire in 2019 and reopened in 2024.

PASTRIES

The pastries that tourists love to eat include millefeuille, religieuse and lemon tart. They are good to eat on a bench in the Tuileries Garden.

LITTLE DANCER, AGED FOURTEEN

A 98-cm-tall statuette sculpted by Edgar Degas between 1878 and 1881, originally in wax, then cast in bronze and dressed in tulle and silk.

VENUS DE MILO

A 2-metre-high marble statue from Milos, carved around 150–125 BCE, on display in the Louvre Museum.

MORRIS COLUMNS

Columns for advertising posters. Their use spread after 1868 thanks to printer Gabriel Morris. There are more than 500 in Paris.

EIFFEL TOWER

World-famous tower by Gustave Eiffel, built in 26 months for the 1889 World Exhibition; it is made up of more than 18,000 iron parts.

WALLACE FOUNTAINS

Public drinking fountains which appeared in Paris in 1872, thanks to philanthropist Sir Richard Wallace, who financed them.

VENICE (Italy)

On the shores of the Adriatic Sea in northeastern Italy, this city is situated on 118 small islands. Canals replace streets, and the Venetians move around in gondolas. From the Middle Ages to the Renaissance, Venice was both a major commercial power and a centre of artistic activity. The city is a jewel of architecture on stilts, with over 450 bridges and countless churches, whose bell towers can be seen from far away, and palaces with richly decorated facades.

MARRAKECH (Morocco)

Located between the Atlantic Ocean and the Atlas Mountains in North Africa, Marrakech is the city that gave its name to the kingdom of Morocco. It has a unique 11th-century medina surrounded by medieval walls. It is a UNESCO World Heritage site with many riads, souks (markets), mosques, gardens, squares and a palm grove of almost 100,000 trees! The red colour of the rock used for its buildings gave it the nickname of the 'ochre city'.

ST MARK'S CAMPANILE
Square tower dating from the 12th century. It towers over Venice at a height of almost 100 metres.

VENICE CARNIVAL
Traditional festival dating back to the Middle Ages, it has been used as a celebration for lots of different things. It is now one of the world's biggest celebrations.

VAPORETTO
Water bus for getting around on the city's canals or to islands in the lagoon which are inaccessible by land.

KUTUBIYYA
A 12th-century structure built in pink sandstone for Abd al-Mu'min, Berber caliph (leader) of the Almohad dynasty. This royal family owned many architectural jewels.

VILLA MAJORELLE
Created by Jacques Majorelle between 1922 and 1931, this house and its beautiful grounds were bought by Yves Saint Laurent and Pierre Bergé in 1980.

ROYAL PALM GROVE
A 15,000-hectare oasis planted in the 11th century for Yūsuf ibn Tāshufīn, sultan and founder of Marrakech around 1065.

RIALTO BRIDGE
The oldest footbridge in Venice, once made of wood and rebuilt in stone by architect and engineer Antonio da Ponte in the late 16th century.

DOGE'S PALACE
The first palace was built in 814. It once contained Venetian political institutions and was the home of the doge, elected ruler of Venice.

ST MARK'S LION
Emblem of Venice and symbol of St Mark the Evangelist, patron saint of the city, whose relics are in the Basilica of St Mark.

ZELLIGE
Small pieces of coloured ceramic used for decorative mosaics which were extremely popular from the 14th century onwards, under the reign of the Marinids.

ORANGE TREE
Symbol of the Marrakech landscape, its spring flowers provide delicious flavours for Moroccan cuisine.

MINT TEA
Traditionally served by men, people in Marrakech drink mint tea several times a day.

SEAGULLS
There are so many of these in Venice that they are chased away with water pistols.

PURPLE ARTICHOKE
The vineyard-covered island of Sant'Erasmo supplies the lagoon's residents with its famous purple artichokes.

GELATO
Italian ice cream, made with milk, which gives it a light, velvety texture.

LANTERN
Metalworking is widespread in Morocco. Wrought-iron lanterns are part of this artisanal heritage.

JOUTIA ZRABI
This market is one of the many souks in the city. It specialises in selling traditionally made Moroccan carpets.

WHITE STORK
When cold winter weather reaches Europe, this wading bird migrates to warmer countries in search of food. It stops to rest in Marrakech, sometimes spending the winter here.

VERA DA POZZO
Many of the city's squares and palace courtyards have their own well with a beautifully decorated carved rim. More than 6,000 were built in the Middle Ages, but only 600 remain today.

GONDOLA
Venetian flat-bottomed boat in use since the 11th century, rowed with a single oar by a gondolier who stands in the rear of the boat.

GUERRAB
Travelling water seller, dressed in a vibrant costume. This traditional trade is gradually disappearing.

MOUCHARABIEH
Openwork window or partition first built in the 13th century, to bring air inside buildings, reduce sunlight and allow people to see out without being seen!

ORANGE JUICE CARTS
There are many of these, all on the Jemaa el-Fna square selling orange juice for a few dirhams.

BAMAKO (Mali)

Bamako is the capital city of Mali and is located on the banks of the Niger River. In Mali, 'bamako' means 'crocodile river'. Mali's capital is home to around 3 million inhabitants. They come from a variety of ethnic groups, and many languages are spoken in the country, including Bambara, Bobo, Mamara and Malinke.

ISTANBUL (Turkey)

This city was one of the capitals of the ancient world, along with Rome and Athens. At one time called Byzantium, then Constantinople, it wasn't until the 15th century that the Turks took it back from the Romans and gave it its current name. Straddling Europe and Asia, it is situated on the shores of the Bosphorus, the strait that links the Black Sea to the Sea of Marmara. Its history and geographical location make it a multicultural city with a unique style of architecture.

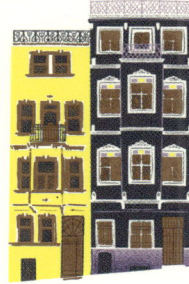

SOTRAMAS
Public transport minibus, that is very popular with Bamako residents due to its low fares.

TASSALÉ
A kind of traditional kettle, also known as séli-daga, used for washing.

MONOBLOC CHAIR
You can see these plastic chairs everywhere on the streets of Bamako. They are very popular throughout the world.

BALAT DISTRICT
A Jewish quarter until the mid-20th century, there are five synagogues, but also several churches and mosques.

WHIRLING DERVISHES
Started as a form of meditation in the 13th century, the dervishes (dancers) wear white robes and spin round.

BLUE MOSQUE
Built in the 17th century during the reign of Sultan Ahmed I, it has six minarets and around 20,000 blue ceramic tiles.

PINK MARKET
Bamako's large souk, which opened in the 20th century, has kept its original style, despite frequent fires.

BOUYE JUICE
Juice from the fruit of the baobab, highly valued by Malians. It is well-known for its nutritional value.

PIROGUE
Long, narrow wooden boat propelled by a paddle or sail, often used on the River Niger.

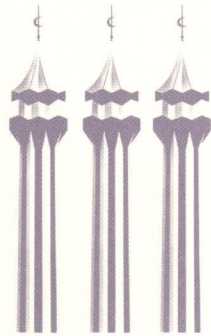

TASBIH
String of beads, often made of wood and also called 'misbaha', used by Muslims during prayer.

VAPUR
Public steamboat, which sails on the Bosphorus between Turkey's European and Asian shores.

EVIL EYE
An amulet to ward off the evil eye, sometimes still made by traditional glassmakers.

KING FAISAL BIN ABDULAZIZ MOSQUE
Built in 1976, originally named Bamako Grand Mosque but renamed in 2017.

PEACE MONUMENT
Opened in the 1990s, the giant arms hold up a globe with a white dove perched on top; it symbolises national unity and the return of peace to Mali.

INDEPENDENCE MONUMENT
A symbol of freedom built in 1995, topped by two domes made from bronze from Mali, designed by architect Amadou Sidibé.

TRAMWAY
The tram is one of the easiest modes of transport in Istanbul. It has 3 lines.

TOPKAPI PALACE
Once home to the Ottoman rulers, starting with Mehmed II, it is now a museum and has an extensive collection of books and manuscripts.

BASILICA CISTERN
Underground reservoir with 336 columns, built in the sixth century by order of Emperor Justinian I.

CROCODILES
Three Caiman crocodiles on the city's coat of arms represent the three rivers flowing through Bamako.

DJEMBÉ
Carved from wood and topped with an animal skin, percussionists use this goblet-shaped drum to play traditional Malian music.

HAIR BEADS
Made of carved wood, engraved terracotta, copper, silver or bronze, Malian women use these little beads to decorate their plaited hairstyles.

TULIP FESTIVAL
Annual event held in April for this flower that won the hearts of the Ottomans in the 11th century, long before it arrived in Europe.

SIMIT
Ring-shaped bread roll, widespread in Turkey for several centuries. There are similar versions in Greece and Armenia.

CAT
There are tens of thousands of these felines in the city's streets.

JAIPUR (India)

The pink city of Jaipur is in northern India, in the state of Rajasthan. It gets its name from its creator, the Maharaja Sawai Jai Singh II. Passionate about astronomy, in the 18th century he ordered the construction of a highly accurate observatory, and then the city, according to a strict geometric design. Inside the city walls there are several luxuriously decorated palaces painted pink!

LOTUS GATE
One of the four gates of the City Palace, dating from 18th century, decorated with lotus petals and dedicated to the god Shiva.

MARIGOLD
Flower associated with most Hindu religious ceremonies, offered to the gods and believed to ward off evil spirits.

PATRIKA GATE
Jaipur's ninth gate, with nine arches, made up of a variety of shapes. It demonstrates the essence of Rajasthan's architectural heritage.

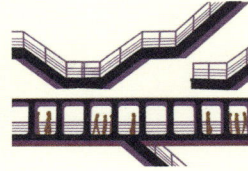

PANNA MEENA KA KUND
Stepwell criss-crossed with many stairs, dug to collect rainwater in the 6th century.

MAKAR SANKRANTI
Festival held in mid-January, linked to the sun and the zodiac, celebrated with many events, particularly kite-flying competitions.

AUTO RICKSHAW
Three-wheeled motorised vehicle that is often used as a taxi.

JAIPUR BLUE POTTERY
Traditional pottery made from quartz, which gets its brilliant blue colour from cobalt blue pigments.

JANTAR MANTAR
Open-air astronomical observatory built in the early 18th century for Maharaja Jai Singh II. It has a set of around 20 main fixed instruments.

KATHPUTLI
String puppet theatre that originated over 1000 years ago. The puppets are usually carved and painted by the puppeteers themselves.

HAWA MAHAL
Palace of the Winds, built in pink sandstone. It is 15 metres high, with five storeys and 953 windows. Completed in 1799 by order of Maharaja Sawai Pratap Singh.

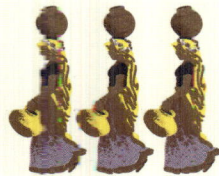

SARI
Women's clothing made from a piece of fabric several metres long. It can be draped in different ways.

LANGUR
Small monkey that lives in large groups and often invades towns. The groups in Jaipur live in the Amber Fort, among other places.

HONG KONG (China)

Located on China's southern coast, Hong Kong is one of the richest cities in the world, but also one of the most crowded. It has more skyscrapers than New York City, and it's not uncommon for several lanes to overlap on the same street to allow vehicles and pedestrians to travel without too many traffic jams! It is a cosmopolitan city, with its own currency, the Hong Kong dollar.

ELEVATED CENTRAL WALKWAY
Network of elevated walkways built in the 1970s to make it easier for people to walk between buildings.

GOLDEN BAUHINIA
A 6-metre-high sculpture of a golden Bauhinia x blakeana flower presented by China to mark the city being handed back by the UK in 1997.

PAVILION OF ABSOLUTE PERFECTION
Gold-covered pagoda, in the style of the Tang dynasty, built in the traditional garden of Nan Lian.

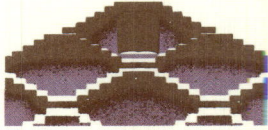

CHOI HUNG ESTATE
Residential district dating from the 1960s, known for its rainbow-coloured blocks of flats.

GOLDFISH MARKET
A street of stalls selling tropical fish and other aquatic animals and aquarium items.

RED MINIBUS
Unlike the green minibuses which follow precise routes and have fixed schedules, red minibuses are more flexible.

BANK OF CHINA HEAD-QUARTERS
A 367-metre-high glass and aluminium skyscraper completed in 1989 by architect I.M. Pei.

TIAN TAN BUDDHA
Statue completed in 1993, 34 metres high and made up of 202 bronze pieces placed onto a steel structure.

FORMER KOWLOON-CANTON RAILWAY CLOCK TOWER
A 44-metre-high neo-Edwardian style tower built in 1915.

LION DANCE
Traditional dance performed by two dancers wearing one lion costume, performed as part of Lunar New Year celebrations.

TRAMWAY
The island's tram network is made up of 6 main routes and 120 stations.

JUNK
Traditional seagoing boat with two or three masts. Its sails are often red and have horizontal frames made from bamboo.

TOKYO (Japan)

Japan is an archipelago of several thousand islands in the Pacific Ocean. The capital, Tokyo, is on the largest island, Honshū. Situated on the eastern side of Mount Fuji, it began as a fishing village called Edo. It flourished in the 17th century, attracting craftspeople, merchants and samurai, under the governance of shōgun (general) Tokugawa. In 1868, it was taken over by Emperor Meiji and renamed Tokyo. Today, the city extends far beyond its historic centre and is one of the most highly populated cities in the world!

SYDNEY (Australia)

Sydney is located in the state of New South Wales, on Australia's east coast. It's the largest city in Australia and has one of the most important ports in the South Pacific. The city is the economic heart of Australia. Sydney's iconic landmarks, the Sydney Opera House and Harbour Bridge, along with its stunning beaches, have become world-famous!

SHIBUYA
A lively district known for its art, fashion boutiques and its huge crossroads crowded with pedestrians.

TŌRŌ
Lantern made of stone, wood or metal, which came from China, originally used in Buddhist temples in Japan.

JIHANKI
Vending machine for drinks, fruit and newspapers. There are millions of them in Japan, in a wide variety of designs.

THE ROCKS
A historic district in Sydney, which was built by the first European settlers in 1788.

VEGEMITE™
Savoury spread, developed in 1922 by Cyril P. Callister to rival Marmite™.

LUNA PARK
Historic Art Deco-style amusement park, opened to the public in 1935 by American entrepreneur Herman Phillips.

MEIJI-JINGŪ SHRINE
Founded in 1920, this shrine is located in a large forest, in the middle of Tokyo.

KAMINARIMON
Thunder Gate, through which you pass to reach Sensō-ji, Tokyo's oldest temple, founded in the 7th century.

HACHIKŌ
Bronze statue of a famous faithful dog.

WHITE SEAHORSE
Seahorse native to Australia's east coast, living in the sea around Sydney. Habitat loss threatens it with extinction.

SYDNEY OPERA HOUSE
Designed by architect Jørn Utzon and opened in 1973, this marvel of engineering welcomes over 10 million visitors every year.

SAKURA
Ornamental cherry tree. Every spring during the Hanami festival, people go to see the cherry blossom and celebrate its beauty.

MOUNT FUJI
Active volcano and sacred mountain, situated at the highest point in Japan at an altitude of 3,776 metres. Although it's 100 km from Tokyo, you can see it on a clear day.

MANEKI NEKO
Ceramic or porcelain ornament of a seated cat raising a paw to welcome visitors and bring good luck.

FERRY
In Sydney, people take the ferry as often as a bus or underground train. It's sometimes faster than using the bridge to reach the opposite shore.

SYDNEY HARBOUR BRIDGE
Bridge crossing Sydney Harbour and built in 1932 by architect and engineer John Bradfield.

TOWER EYE
Opened in 1981, this panoramic tower has 420 windows. Including its telecommunications spire, it's 309 metres high.

DARUMA
Papier-mâché figurine believed to symbolise good luck and perseverance.

RAMEN
Delicious Japanese noodle soup, often topped with a boiled egg.

SURF
Sydney's beaches are famous for their perfect waves. Surfers flock there from all over the world.

HORNBY LIGHTHOUSE
Lighthouse measuring over 9 metres tall. Designed by architect Alexander Dawson and built in 1858 after a tragic shipwreck.

SCRIBBLY GUM TREE
Eucalyptus tree from the Sydney region, identifiable by the 'scribbles' on its bark, which are actually caterpillar tracks.

KOINOBORI
Windsocks in the shape of colourful koi carp, traditionally put up on 5 May to celebrate Children's Day.

TOKYO TOWER
A 333-metre-high metal telecommunications tower completed in 1958.

COCOON TOWER
Its full name is Mode Gakuen Cocoon Tower, located in the Shinjuku district.

CAMDEN MARKET
DOMINO PARK
ONE WAY
TELEPHONE
AVENIDA 5 DE MAYO
PLACE DES VOSGES
ЛАВРУШИНСКИЙ
ПЕРЕУЛОК